My Poet's Tongue

MADDIE VEE

My Poet's Tongue

Copyright © 2020 by Maddie Vee

All rights reserved by the author. No part of this book may be used or reproduced or transmitted in any form or by any electronic means including photocopying, recording, or by storage in any retrieval system without the written permission from the author.

Disclaimer

The contents of this book should be used for information only. The author, affiliate organizations and publisher assume no responsibility for any decision made as a result of reading this book that can affect your business or personal life.

1st Printing

ISBN: 978-1-7343699-0-8

Printed in the United States of America

DEDICATION

Dedicated to My Father Nelson Velez May Poetry live beyond us.

To my Mother Evelyn Torres and her unwavering faith, friendship, and mercy.

To My Daughter Annabelle Eve who at 5yrs old doesn't quite understand she is my story "the dream" everything after her is the cherry on top, never stop being curious.

To my eldest Niece Joeylyn Nicole, know that our love is unshakably ours, don't stop writing.

Finally, to the little girl kept away in the cupboard, you are now free.

Dedicado a mi Padre Nelson Velez Que viva el poeta que no descansa hasta encontrar libertad con su pluma.

Para mi madre Evelyn Torres por su Amor y Amistad.

FOREWORD

Hello, my name is Emilio Roman and I am the Publisher of the Bestselling book series Spiritual Fitness Survivor as well as an International Award-Winning Bestseller Author.

I have had the opportunity to encounter many talented individuals as I travel throughout the United States and abroad. I always stop and listen to my intuition when someone's work is different than my own. Maddie's genre certainly qualifies as polar opposite.

It is with immense pleasure that I write this foreword on behalf of a very talented and driven individual Maddie Vee. I enjoyed the honor of connecting with her parents at a private function not too long ago.

I was very fascinated and wanted to learn more about this local poet. Fast forward a few weeks later and her parents presented me with a copy of Maddie's book. The very next day we had a meeting. Her style of poetry and view of the world are incredibly intriguing. It became apparent early in our conversation; Maddie has been through many challenges in her life. Her poetry represents a beneficial way for her to express her feelings and to heal from those challenges.

I soon discovered Maddie's style of writing is raw and unlike any other I have ever experienced. Her very deep words send a clear message to your soul of the struggles she has endured.

Maddie has written her book A Poet's Tongue in the style of a modern-day Chapbook. Chapbooks were small booklets sold by chapmen in 16th century Europe and the United Kingdom. Chapmen otherwise known as peddlers or hawkers sold their goods at fairs, markets, on street corners or door to door.

I think you will discover this a fascinating collection of poetry transporting you on a journey through Maddie Vee's life.

Emilio Roman
Publisher - Spiritual Fitness Survivor

WHAT IS A CHAPBOOK?

This little book is a modern-day Chapbook. What is a Chapbook? These small booklets first appeared in 16th century Europe. They were sold by chapmen, otherwise known as peddlers or hawkers selling their wares at fairs, markets, on street corners or door to door.

Chapbooks were a significant way to circulate popular culture to ordinary people, particularly those living in the country side. The underprivileged and children were likely most of their readers. They were cheap entertainment or informational and typically provided readers with fiction such as fairy tales, ghost stories, poetry, ballads, or non-fiction such as news coverage on politics crime or disasters, etc.

Today these short, artfully designed books have remained as an attractive method for poets and writers who want to reach niche audiences using small press publishers.

TABLE OF CONTENTS

DEDICATION 5

FOREWORD 7

WHAT IS A CHAPBOOK? 9

    She Hides Me 13

    Not Me 14

    ARRRGGH Mati 16

    Curiosity Kills Hunger 17

    Never Again 18

    I Can Hear Him 19

    One Day, Starts Like Everyday 20

    Beautiful 22

    Mundane Day 25

    Poet's Hunger 26

    Living Poets 27

    Man 101 29

    Where Science Ends, God begins, and She Leaves 31

    Pretend 33

    Ordinarily Unique 34

    Recycled Words 35

    Mother 37

Drowning Offspring 39

Predictions...41

The Other Side Less Greener 42

Songs of Solomon 8:6 43

Camden – September 24th 2014 44

And Then You'll Live 46

The Words are always ticking (Aug 2014) 48

Hibernation 49

A false Win 50

Tomorrow...51

Tin Man 52

God's Listening..53

3:00 am Black Veil Mass 54

February 17..55

New Skin (Motherhood) 56

The Calmness of Pain 57

A Forever At Least Once 58

She Hides Me

She hides me like an old tire worn down and flat piled in the yard and hidden
One day I'll run into someone who is not afraid or ashamed of my scars, but today that's not her.
Her love lives on the surface wide open curtains, that are afraid to open the skies and realize that my yelling has led somewhere.
Somewhere safe into the chaos.
She loves me in print form every letter holding itself up on paper, but I prefer more.
She looks at me like I've just murdered myself, like butchered meat on the hook
like I'm the Joker.
I'm so beautiful in between the shadows where the imperfections are not highlighted, but I'm not as beautiful by her sun.
She loves me like her best Sharpened knives, the ones she's been holding onto for years
and doesn't know why, I'm the question mark at the end of her question.
But I prefer more.
Am I crazy enough to want more?
An emotion produced and provoked from true harmonious conversations.
Rattled by my skin she hiss's her deceit into me and I slither away.

Not Me

The roll of the dice does not scare you as much as where it could land you are afraid of me and if not then your posture sure is. I exist only in front of your eyes but with a turning of the head I evaporate from thoughts and die away. Only I don't buy your shit you resuscitate me in the shower and berate me with your palm you dirty bastard, as corrupt as my many fluctuating sins. Humanity ties us together in golden wired thread. The equivalent of a toddler toiling away at his mother's breast, you are bonded by survival to the nature of my way. God damn it I've never felt this way.

He's convinced himself that I'm confused, that I have debris falling off my tongue and that I've placed my dreamy eyes in jars of honey that my smile is dripping wet from needing and wanting. As if a stuffed bag of validation sat in his back pocket to abuse my naivety. As if I'm bargaining my innocence away. I smile because I have sharper knives, and no one knows where they lay. Do not be deceived, no one knows who comes in the door until they leave. He believes he's in control, but his tongue is disobedient and betrays him. I could catch all of him in a Sippy cup and sit him on my shelf to age.

He isn't exactly running from me, in fact he's running towards, so confused, needing much of things I already have. He says love pointed away from me but he says it pointing away from himself. He knows not what he says he is knotted up in friction. So much static in his head his hair can't lay down. He says we are the same in so many ways, but I truly don't see it maybe my ego won't settle to be compared to a confused man, maybe there is more in common but from here the clouds are hiding him away. I don't see how we could ever be similar but maybe.

He looks as if he's appeared from my grandmother's garden with the wild thorns still stuck to him he is warm a tropical mango palette of flavors I can only assume taste sweet. He hides himself in such a clumsy way he trips over himself, and thinks I am the one falling.
A man, no one would guess could be this way, but damn it, how could they not it's all there, between his brows on the cress of his round dime shaped eyes. He's there loudly how could you not see such a funny little thing.

If he is truly anything like me even an ounce then here it ends playfully, gliding to its death 101 fucked up thoughts burning a hole inside of every desire to end in a Disney dream. Maybe that's why I hope he's not me.

ARRRGGH Mati

Sometimes I just want to sit on a feeling
Indulge in my mortality
Feel the things that burst from my insides and learn them
Master myself in a wicker chair and a melting sun
Be at peace with my pains
Hear no words and be ok with it
And I need you to be ok with it to
Sometimes I want to wonder about everything and get no answers
I'm traveling through myself in ways I cannot share
God has scrapped my tongue off I'm purging my sins and he keeps the words
and I can't give what I don't have
sometimes my silence isn't a mystery
just a conversation with all of my buried treasures
tomorrow we can build sandcastles again.

Curiosity Kills Hunger

My curiosity is dwindling but there's still enough to write about.

Throwing his virginity out of his mouth to the carpet a sweet surrender propelling to its floor.

 So early so intimate so loud in front of the world and he looks away how much of you can be met at 7:30 a.m. how much of me is listening really.

Strangers with knotted tongues but as a June bud that I am I flutter away still intrigued. Knowing he could not have all of me.

After he scrapped his tongue, all those unused words would be given to the next pretty girl that caught his eye, and I don't have an empty jar for gouging, two round dimed eyes.

Never Again

Time is a thief
I'm not angry at aging
a body does what it must through the years and it does its job well for me
every year I collect is a year deducted from them
every year she is less mine and more of the world
I haven't spoken to him in years no part of my childhood is preserved
alone is something that awaits me
I love these people not only because we are tied and weaved through natures approval
But
because I genuinely like the way they are, mine
every piece built to sooth me and every piece I have caters to them
in bliss, anger, destruction, tranquility, and faith
Never again is terrifying.

I Can Hear Him

I would love to breathe again
And yes, I can hear him
His applause with both bottom and top lip
I can hear him hearing me
I know the silence he carries when just outside that door he's listening
To my dreams unfold
And he's taking that journey I sell so well
But I believe in the magic too
I can see him through every word I spill
And until I hear that last step down the stairs
I know I must preform
Because he's listening to my words
And I'm listening to his silence
And we are healing each other's poverty with hope
I wonder if he misses my voice and still stands by that window listening for more.
Knowing that I will never be back again.

One Day, Starts Like Everyday

One day I asked myself, after watching the world curl up and hide itself under social media posts and scripted relationships, what is it?

What is that one thing that could bury you even now, even tomorrow what is the worst human emotion to me?
Abandonment,
It frightens you
In a way that your teeth tremble and your empty
Like an October pumpkin
Hallow inside but with a smile on the outside

Seeing someone leave is like standing at the edge of the field and knowing that although harvest was great this year hardships are to come
You can see that these seeds won't meet a good spring
That turning your face is the safest thing to do but you can't because there are still pumpkins sprouting from the ground, and pumpkin soup sounds good and pumpkin spice cookies sound comforting and there are too many recipes for me to go hungry until I run out , but I know once I look back the field will wither, and not even one of my tears could bring its glory back to me.
Abandonment is playing pretend.

Soothing an ache that has proclaimed its residency within you.
A roommate you didn't want but can't afford to let go
A surprise visit that will never leave
Abandonment feels worse than getting whipped by a thousand leather belts
Or scrapping your knee as you fell off the bike
Abandonment is you never coming back
Either by choice or not
It leaves you hallow
And running and always afraid
And always remembering
Anticipating
Not much can dismember that one goodbye.

Beautiful

It's not that I hate him
It's that he still hurts
He's still peeling off of me
I never believed anything beyond today
But I wanted to believe
Now that Cinderella has been ruined
I'm back to a dim reality
Where ghetto girls could never be more then what they are
Challenged, bruised, angry, and repulsive to an outside world that doesn't include food stamps and broken railings, graffiti poets preaching the sermons in community library's
And although strong never considered someone's wife
No one marries here out of love
Only need
We're all starving, and no one ever gets enough
Pretty enough for a ghetto girl
 I think that's their thought
I wish I could draw curtains on my city, so the outside couldn't come in
With their bullshit handouts and their practice of empathy
Their ticket to heaven
"The outside people coming in to save us"

Their far more damaging then the realities that plague us
There is still love here
Even if to them we are profits
A coin to be flipped
And although we love like school children and run around barefooted
We are still
As beautiful
Some ghetto girls still dream into adulthood a Disney dream
so, fuck the outside world
For not understanding our survival
If I was born to be underprivileged in society's standard
Then don't tell me I'll be anything else, keep Cinderella in her cellar
Don't tell me that a poor maid arrived at a fucking ball in a pumpkin and become someone's wife
If all I'll ever ride is the bus
Don't tell me that after being poisoned by an apple a girl can wake up to magical kiss
When only the opposite could happen to me, when waking up with pieces missing is my reality
Prince charming is a rapist.
Don't tell me that a mermaid can walk on land to join a world in bliss all because of love
Because the outside coming in is never a good idea

My Poet's Tongue

As much as the winds whistles your poor your broken
your never as beautiful
We ghetto girls
feed those suburban kids that dress nice
And know how to fucking use a salad fork and know the
difference between them both
Our poverty feeds America
And with full belly's They spit at us.

Mundane Day

These days every word seems to be piling up on one another before the last sentence of my first thought can be formed completely, I hear clear across the tracks another approaching. I guess things are hectic, or I can't just keep up with myself on a normal day. Maybe now I'm just realizing that. The neighbor's laugh's sound like farm hens clucking away only I wish they were fenced in with chicken wire. The city is barely alive. There are not many conversations floating about everyone is tucked away into corners. Only a couple of mindless chuckles and people exchanging exclusive thoughts with eye flickering attempts. Everything seems piled up.

Poet's Hunger

I buy more dreams then I do Clothes
Their half priced but still too expensive
I'd buy gum
But it's like nicotine
There's something about it
That calms me
I exchange thoughts with vital people whose artistic
hearts are still breathing
I exchange dead views in hopes of resuscitating
something grand
Jealous like a priest with his church
I cannot let go of who I am.

Living Poets

That's all were doing validating each other's existence in conversations
Our words don't melt us together,
survival does
at least poetry as I met it
does
Most of us poets don't write for accolades
We're just breathing it happens to sound alluring to non-poets
But we write for each other
To know we are not the only ones walking backwards
To chuckle at the insanity that other's rave "was so beautifully put"
We puree their truths and lay them warm for supper
And they don't care about our hunting seasons
I think I know my end
I think you know my end
Satan isn't that scary after all
He's a cowardly figure
A pussy cat really
My survival is appeasing your adventurer
never forget I am drinking your poison
we are truly a small breed
a tightly wounded circle that doesn't want to meet on Sundays
And you are welcome

My Poet's Tongue

To much of me is given to you
But I don't give two shits about a thank you
These are not performances
These are not performances
These are not performances
I am the poet
the spectator
the audience
the nun flustered at mass
I'm the in between of sleep
the roaring 5yr old meeting mortality
We are all of these things without your permission
We are sleeping aides collecting dreams we can't sit on.

Man 101

How I feel with him is almost the same way I feel without him
His steps are there like a smoldering heat rising before me
 I'm so mesmerized and tortured by it
That I run in place
My pulse is aching my body into shame
And no limb wants to take credit, but I know it's not in me to feel this way
I guess this is what love feels like in words
And this is what it all sounds like in motion
 this is what my body is speaking
Everything about the day seems perfect
It's yellow, a happy color that paints on spring
Merry in cinnamon like the first winter days where your excited for Christmas
7 days of joy
It's a great conversation when eyes to eyes meet
Every other body part wants to follow
It. He places me back into a world where I love to know I exist
He reminds me that I exist
And too be happy
It's effortless
To love
It's uninvited

My Poet's Tongue

Like a mystic wind violently bursting into you
With fall leaves and birthday candles
It feels like magic again
Pony rides and sidewalk chalk
Cherry water ice and summer breaks
No surrender no fear
I'm laying my head down in familiar places that I've never quite experienced
But knew I would get too
like his hands, I knew they would come
And his smile, I knew he would feel jolly like December
An inch away is too far for me
But the truth is he's not mine
He's not here for me
He came here with full hands and empty eyes
And it was all unintended and uninvited
But we escaped each other
As luck would have it. Not even a hello made a way between us.

Where Science Ends, God begins, and She Leaves

Laying raw and red inside
It's like I'm rolling a human dice
I'm sweating like I'm bewitched by demons
Swaying my body from dark shadow to dark shadow
You could not survive me
I can barely survive me
From time to time
My body disconnects from itself
And reality is merely an illusion
The pain is stubborn and stuck
I regurgitate everything and all I sing is mercy, mercy, mercy
It does all ache inside
My muscles are tightly wounded, and every part scared
On the other side from the howling and gasps and moans the ones that scare even the throat that's providing the symphony sounds
There is someone at the end
Standing in murky shadows by a lamppost under an umbrella
Waiting to resuscitate me again
She's waiting terrified because I know she is
But with a calm I love you, stance
One that only a mother can give
And she waits till I find life again

My Poet's Tongue

She waits singing a hopeful hymn
A silent tune only I and she hear
I wonder if
Sometimes
One day
There will be just an umbrella at the end
Well then,
No life is spared that breaths
And that is what I remind myself when I sing mercy mercy mercy
I'll just have to bury myself dead after all.

Pretend

Everything breaths color, death itself lays on a concrete
goodbye the color itself fades on your eyes
And we are all going to fly
While color blind
Nothing trumps these lies
That color is everlasting a truthful hymn because even
the blind can see the trouble in men
And that flesh fades and there will be nothing more
When death shallows at our squeaky door
And all the colors will be no more
After you unlock that treacherous door
We will hear our shouts galore
To the Lord, to the Lord
And our mouths will dry
The rich will be poor
Because all the glittery things will not fit past that door
And all the tongues will scramble in a pot, they will boil
to an end
Until enemies learn themselves friends
As we all walk towards the end and there will be no
coming again,
Farewell farewell to all the men
The ones in the light and the ones that pretend.

Ordinarily Unique

The sun looked like it was trying to burn a hole
through my window this morning
Half of me wished it did
I thought it was trying to peep through the curtain
But then it seemed like an angry stalker who wasn't
fulfilled with just a glance
And it stood there
All complete
And behind my morning
In front of my window
And chasing after me hungry
Annoyed I turned away and outside
I noticed it had gone back up to the sky
I thought it was something worth mentioning
It's not every day the sun pays me a visit.

Recycled Words

These lawyers sit upstairs of the pizzeria laughing and laying down phrases like court ordered on the cold upper level of an Italian pizzeria so Italian that Consuelo makes them so Italian that Julio and Davon are the ones inserting and taking out the big hot oven palates with pizza slices at the tip.
Upstairs just leads to the cold
If you were ever curious of where I am today
At 22 in Camden
But Nothing here is special
But I am here
 Nov 20th
I am geographically here
And I'm eating fries with ketchup and a thin long split in the middle garlic stick with pepperoni and cheese in the middle on the upper level
And it's really, cold
And I feel like sharp little pins are being stabbed in my heart randomly, my heart has a long way to go before it gives out, so I'm not worried
But it surprises me, and it hurts
The preppy white long nosed men old with their worn-out hair, and that darker one but still American white, and the one with the cane left with this phrase
"The first man who answers honestly loses"
Which one? I don't know
They all kept down the stairs

My Poet's Tongue

But I'm taking that phrase and sticking it in my pocket
I'm so faithful to honesty maybe a breakup is in order
I'm wearing black and white and a blue scarf
The booths upstairs are burgundy red with details, swirls kind of in gold
I'm alone
I love justice maybe that's why I'm not a lawyer
Don't ever come here for glamour if it still stands here after me
It's not paradise here
But I stand here
Even in a place like this some words can be caught
Recycled words can erupt so many avalanches
And God has me.
But today I'm cold and I'm leaving.

Mother

I want to raise children as tall as the empire state building
I don't want able legs for my children
I want bionic strength
Steady steal armor ripping through the wind
I want them a step ahead from the blade runner
But for them to fall way behind in thoughts
I want them to carry titanium boulders on each arm that
Achilles could only hold in theory

And it starts by saying hello
Hello, I'm your mother bending hips to sway in its most natural form extending legs like edible branches crackling in a hospital bed
Remember before you were ever a part of this world
Before you feed off of grains and soils and milk
You wore me
and I was you're most expensive robe
I wished dreams into you
And I dreamed for you
I set out shouts of praise in between the clouds to reach for you
And I held you captive with gestors of strength
Because before you meet the world you first had to meet me your mother
And before you set out into the world

My Poet's Tongue

Before it attempts to bend you on your knees
Know you are your mother's daughter
 Make no mistake of who you are
You are tethered to this boiling red blood of mine
You come from a praying woman from a sharp tongue and an angry fist
Do not allow foolery to blind you with gold
I have been your most expensive robe
Say proudly I have a single mother
See the goal is not to give you more then enough things although you've been blessed
The trick is to give you enough words
Because milk runs out
Petty people make pretty things fall so quickly and, you are beautiful
But beauty won't keep that smile on
The world will try to turn you off like a light switch
And that my dear is when you come get your mother.

Drowning Offspring

If a ripped flower from its garden can be loved, then I am loved too
It is also dying in front of your window
God is a fluid conversation smeared on our lips and you have the audacity to smack them against me
Their eyes lit up, rosy cheeks, nose in the air
If you rip me from the roots that fed me I'll surely still survive
Until I expire, that is
I'm still feeding from the world ten thousand sick sorrows that have unraveled from your palms
Sustaining myself with tomorrows is questioning the ability of our today

They love me
I'm sure they do somehow

But chained into a blurred memory is where they've buried me
where roses are endless, and I'm always tied up and tethered to disgrace
 bewitched into a trance trailing off into a foreign tongue
into a whisper they cannot hear I plead mercy for my sinners
My blood is no different

My Poet's Tongue

They know no better than to laugh with an open bible
chuckling with the shadow man
They believe all their lies

as if misery were a place
but griefs on their laps and I don't sit there anymore

I'm always in question

Like my love can't fill their cold tiny hands and my pot
of rice is not enough like every bean is counted
I could bring down the heavens lasso Jesus Christ back
down to me and still they say
But   where   is   God?

Their lips find each other in unfortunate thoughts
 their lungs sprout air at exactly the wrong time

Every arrow pointed to me, the hunters gaze like
predators, like unloved children like their mother
abandoned them but she had to go, without their
permission

They morph from playing children to hungry wilder
beast parading in green skin
What is this feeling they dress themselves in?
Grandma never told me any of this.

Predictions

I love you
Should not be a phrase used in past tense with remorse
Compassion shouldn't be piled up next to the quarters in your back pocket
Yesterday shouldn't bleed into today
And coffee is less bitter when accompanied with someone else
Stories are only good if someone's listening
Kites fly up
Lions are wild and we're the tamed, ones I guess kind of so

I love you
Shouldn't stand next to an I'm sorry it shouldn't brush up against a maybe
Laughter goes great with wine
Picnics go great with friends
Lust and innocence should crave commitment
Lit candles are the best
Penguins mate for a lifetime with only one partner

and most of it never goes that way.

The Other Side Less Greener

Being an object to be moved with a salivating tongue isn't appealing as you've assumed it would be. Everything about your hands offend me. Being admired isn't enough. There may be a lot of things to fake but love is one of those rare things that is or isn't. A solid trinket hanging to you.

Songs of Solomon 8:6

I felt like you were holding the other part of the world
and I mines
But you let go
It feels like My childhood has committed suicide
And I'm struck heartbroken
I think we fall in love with the magic
More so then the people
I think death becomes by pushing all the seasons
together until a light is birthed and we find each other
All at different ends of one thought
And no explanation could make sense of the nonsense
And no one is free from the taunting
And No, I love yous can save our feet from dangling
above the air.

Camden – September 24th 2014

White orchids
Or pink cherry blossoms at my door
A simple verse from a tired labor worker
With rustic hands drenched in oil and paving curious ideas in my head.
That'd be nice to have.
A simple story beginning at the playground to 50 yrs of stories handed down
Church bells
quiet summer's fishing
Holding generations and leading them to love by example.
Meeting by the river
Escorted to the theater
Laughing through hand ornaments and smell of pie in November
That'd be nice.
To bring someone home
To a complete home of mother and father waiting one on the porch and the other by the kitchen.
In looking for a yes and finding it.
To taking little feet to a safe place to learn
That'd be nice.
To have love reach its potential.
Giving it life and receiving it back.

To Wither alongside years of genuine emotion until both
eyelids one after the other find their way
By a cemented fate.
That'd be nice.
But we don't live there.

And Then You'll Live

There is life beyond a point of grief
and there is love, an abundance
Sometimes we just want to leave angry just because it's easier to say he broke my heart
Then to say we tried and failed
Or he was selfish, and he hung to many dreams up to the Sun and I'm dried up from false illusions and he got rid of us
Did Any of that really happen
Or was it that we specifically didn't venture farther then tomorrow
Because 27 years was too much
And hanging his dirty ass underwear was tiresome
And hearing me bitch about shit
Seemed gloomy to him
Because not everyone is designed to carry one another for 20-35 yrs
Not every plate brought to the dinner table is eaten, is it?
But leaving angry seems appropriate
He cheated on me, I think that's it, it had to be
But in all fairness, love or what now feels like love can run out for some
22 years can dry up as easily as 2
There is a point beyond grief

There is a moment where you'll find everything that you
once left for him, or her,
 aside
And that small dick bastard will be a good memory
and that flat chested good for nothing bitch
Will become a bright look into a dark space
That ended.
So, what I'm saying is you'll live.

The Words are always ticking (Aug 2014)

Anyone could fall in love with words
Its the bondage that we plead to
when we surrender to poetry
It can feel,
every single time
like a seductive, innovative way of breathing out
Hurling out desperate desires to reach someone other
than yourself
It's a tricky bitch nonetheless
And sometimes even the most experienced Poet gets
tangled on to a series of unforgettable words
Rendering all their own and almost falling to deep into
someone else's
The words are always ticking
And no good experienced Poet can walk away
Wholeheartedly from a new thought.

Hibernation

I wish life had a resting period like hibernation, for when your soul needed it the most.
Like when your knees creek like an old rusty hinge that's minutes away from swelling itself shut.
Or when your lungs cough up winter through your nasal cavities. I wish I could find a resting place for every limb and every thought. Somewhere warm. If only resting your thoughts could be as easy as ordering off of a menu. I'd have a few goodbyes for appetizers not too many I' saving room for my entrée. I'd have a cup of peace to sooth the weight pilled plate I'll soon have. On my plate a handful of compliments a pillow and a sharp fork in case I woke up before dessert. I wish mental health was an ok thing to mention while passing the salt. I wish a panic attack was a bit more of a causal discussion, and that they, the world would know my safe word was ouchhhhh.

A false Win

You get to have the last word
But I get the rest of you after
When your fist unclenches, and your jaw opens to a quivering tongue
When your ignorance falls flat to your ego and you all crawl back to me,
I still, get to, have, you.

Tomorrow

Good Morning text don't wake me up in the morning
My soul still sleeps away
Almost is like a kinda thing I don't want, and wanting is all we naturally.
I wish I could sit in today's skin forever.
If you're going to be the same person in a different place
Then what's the point of showing up.
If all I do is sleep you away, they what's point of waking up.
With the same tongue on the same side of the same bed.
They'll always be seven tomorrows waiting for us.
Seven tomorrow I'll sleep walk through.

Tin Man

Wonder where his eyes finally end
Each lid cementing their tiresome voyage
A boat fueled by hate floating away from me
How far his age will take him
And how he'd look at 70
Will he be content with goodbye, still
What ornaments has he hung on himself
If even one is in remembrance of me
Wonder what casket they'll pick
And where his bones will lay
If he still loves telescopes and stares in aw at the sky
when the stars are draping us both
Does he wonder about them the way I wonder about him.
Loving him is inevitable,
Even the tin man has love set aside for tomorrow.

God's Listening

They're strangling every word that drops out of my mouth
They have power
Unraveling ever thread knitted carefully by God himself
The earth hears me weeping but it holds me still
it will have no mercy on my tyrants
And life will seek its own vengeance away from me
My hands clean
Their eyes bleed with expected anguish
The waiting can be taunting
So their misery is my joy
I remember and they remember
They will fall from grace and I will fall asleep
As the world digs into them, daggers they remember holding
Don't stain the children, the world will mark you unfit
And God was listening under the pillow, anyways.

3:00 am Black Veil Mass

The devil speaks to me
In a thousand riddles that only I hear
He romanticizes death and disguises himself in my laughter
I have to keep him there sometimes
Sometimes he's stuck and I'm stuck
And there we are.

February 17

Loving me takes courage but loving you takes fury
It takes 7 lonely days in February to remember how alone the world can feel
How no one is listening and how you've peeled to many layers off of me
If I could scrap your sins off of me
I would but February 17th always shows up on the calendar.

New Skin (Motherhood)

This new skin feels too big
Sometimes
It feels adjusted for someone else
Like the pins are still on the sides poking at me
Like the soles of the feet are too thin
Like I'll never grow into it
My smile seems unsure and its slipping away
This skin seems bent out
It seems to have to many patches
And I don't know how to where this face
This body is different
I wouldn't say unbeautiful
But it sure is bigger and foreign
It has peaks and valleys
It's different but not unbeautiful
I like the way thunder is imprinted
Right on the tip of my breast
And the trails that lead to my sides
There's something beautiful here

The Calmness of Pain

It will sit by your bed graveling, tucking itself under you
It sneaks in with no permission and I can't promise heartbreak won't come
As much as you can't promise you won't grow
We think of today because it's in front of us touching our noses
But tomorrow is only a few hours away and it will be that way, always
I can't promise that I will always stand here forever
Because I can't manipulate time in my favor
Make pain your playmate because it will always find you in some

A Forever At Least Once

Those two little eyes pin ponging from every corner
There's something beautiful about children and there's something exquisite about her
Those big booming wide eyes
And those endless lashes
A magical merry go round
I find worlds on her palms and vast fields stretching past my understanding
Wide arms spread around my neck steal handles never letting go
A mothers favorite necklace
I think everyone should have an
 Annabelle
A forever at least once

www.ingramcontent.com/pod-product-compliance
Lightning Source LLC
Chambersburg PA
CBHW030915170426
43193CB00009BA/862